Be Imperfect,
Live Longer

Nobody's perfect, right?
So don't be so hard on yourself!

DR. HOWARD MURAD, M.D.

Wisdom Waters Press
1000 Wilshire Blvd., #1500
Los Angeles, CA 90017-2457

Quantity sales. Special discounts are available on quantity purchases by corporations, associations, and others. For details, contact the "Special Sales Department" at the address above.

Printed in China

ISBN-10: 1-939642-23-X
ISBN-13: 978-1-939642-23-3

First Edition

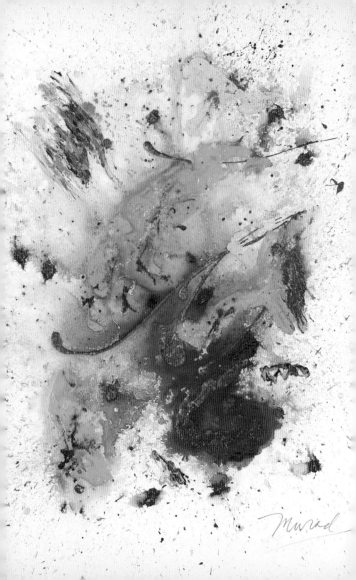

Perfection is an illusion, so don't get caught in the trap of believing that everything you do must be perfect. Strive for excellence instead of perfection, and you'll live a longer and much happier life.

ABOUT
THE ART

Self-expression is essential to human health and happiness. The author was reminded of that several years ago when he discovered a new outlet for his own irrepressible creative drive: painting. Interestingly enough, he's never taken any formal art classes, but his canvases are nonetheless sophisticated. His modernist style makes pure chance a key element in the artistic process. This results in explosions of color and form that expand the limits of imagination. Dr. Murad created the illustrations in this book hoping they would help you expand your imagination and envision a better tomorrow.

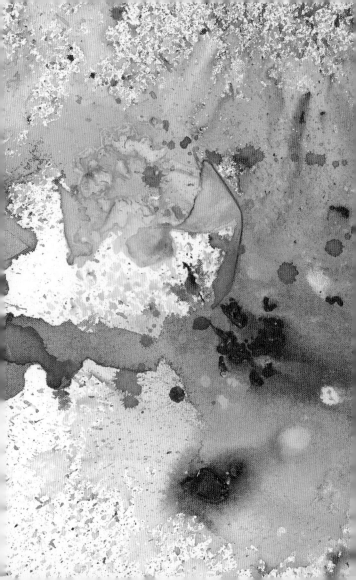

BE IMPERFECT,
LIVE LONGER

I had a dear and beloved aunt who was a wonderful pianist. She could play almost anything—Chopin, Cole Porter, or the latest popular hit—and she always played it well. When she performed for the family, we all watched in amazement as her fingers danced over the keys. If it was Strauss, you could imagine yourself in a symphony hall in Vienna. If it was something from a Broadway musical, you might as well have been sitting in a theater downtown. She really was that good.

It is easy to imagine that with a touch of classical training and a slightly different attitude she might have become a famous concert pianist. Who knows? She might even have performed someday at Carnegie Hall. But it never happened. My aunt was a perfectionist, you see, and no matter how talented they may be, perfectionists almost never reach their full potential.

I still remember the day she sat down at the piano and started in on a Beethoven sonata she'd been trying to master. I've been told that Beethoven sonatas are extremely difficult pieces even for a musician as talented and capable as my aunt, but apparently she felt she was up to the challenge. We all gathered around to listen.

At first it seemed that she was more than a match for this very complicated music. She played it with fire, and those of us listening

10

smiled and nodded our heads in appreciation. Then something happened that none of us had ever seen or heard before. Having reached a particularly demanding passage, my aunt hesitated and stumbled over a few notes. To our shock and surprise, she didn't continue playing but instead sat there at the piano shaking her head and blinking as if she had been hit over the head with a book.

After a few moments, she flexed her fingers and started the piece over from the beginning. She played with renewed determination and vigor, perhaps even more passionately than before, until that is, she reached that same troublesome passage. Again she stumbled, again she stopped in the middle of the piece, and again she started over from the beginning.

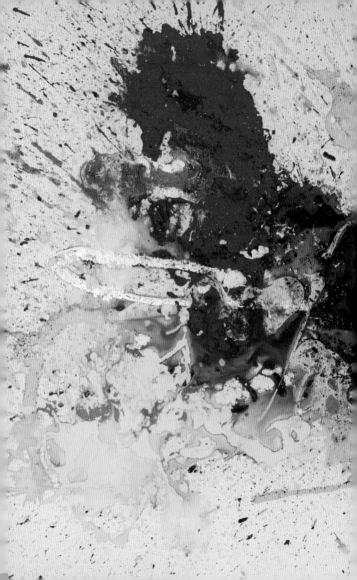

By this time we all realized we were witnessing something truly extraordinary—a confrontation of titanic proportions. It was my aunt against Ludwig van Beethoven. We all held our breath as the critical moment approached. Would she succeed this time?

No! It was unbelievable. She had once again gotten lost in the twisting and turning complexities of the musical lines and, instead of pushing through them as best she could and completing the sonata, she just stopped. She folded up her sheet music and put it away. Then she walked out of the room without a word to anybody.

Here's the strangest part of the story. My aunt never tried to play that piece again—or any other. In fact, she *never* sat down in front of a piano again. This seemingly minor setback had totally deflated her musical ambitions. What a tragedy! Just imagine all the pleasure she denied herself and others simply because she couldn't accept a single instance of failure.

I now understand that my aunt's stumbling block was not that sonata composed so long ago by Beethoven. It had little or nothing to do with any particular musical passage or with the clefts and chords of musical notation. It was also not her nimble fingers that in this one instance had steadfastly refused to do her bidding. Instead, it was in her mind. Her difficulty stemmed from the mistaken and all too common belief that the only acceptable standard of success is perfection.

This is a very destructive notion because people who demand perfection of themselves are doomed to failure—and not just one failure. They are doomed to fail over and over. Why? It's very simple, really. Nobody

14

is perfect, and so nothing we attempt to achieve is ever likely to be perfect either. To put it another way, perfection is an illusion, a mirage that we can never quite reach no matter how hard we try.

Unfortunately, we live in a culture that seems to demand perfection. We are told to strive for perfection and constantly reminded that perfection should always be our goal. But since perfection is impossible, we can never reach that goal and are bound to disappoint ourselves and others.

The damage done by perfectionism doesn't stop with disappointment. When you are a perfectionist, it's hard on you spiritually and emotionally. If you are a perfectionist, you are always asking too much of yourself, which is almost certain to make you unhappy. There are physical consequences as well. When you are unhappy, your brain

15

releases chemicals that can damage your cells and make you sick.

Over the years I've treated thousands and thousands of patients and spent countless hours listening to them describe their symptoms. Inevitably, I've learned a lot about them as individuals—their opinion of themselves, what they thought of their accomplishments, and their view of life in general. I'm struck by how many of them were their own harshest critics. To hear it from them, you'd have thought that nothing they'd ever done was worthy of praise. Of course that wasn't true, but they seemed to think so. Nothing had ever been quite good enough.

Not surprisingly, most people with this sort of negative attitude are unhappy with their lives, with their work, with their relationships, and with themselves. How could

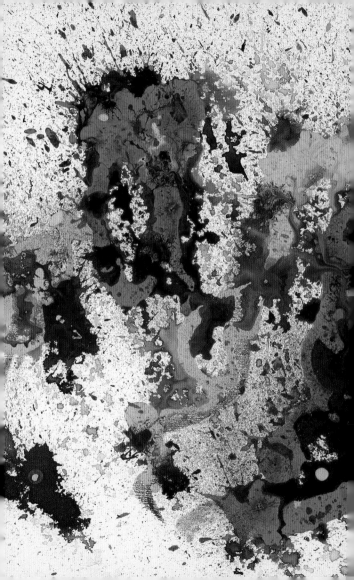

it be otherwise? When you are that hard on yourself all of the time, it's sure to make you unhappy.

Yes, perfectionism makes people unhappy, it makes them sick, and it's a prescription for failure. If everything we do must be perfect, how can we ever succeed? We try to be perfect, but we can't and this convinces us that we are natural-born failures. No one is born to fail. Rather, we are all born to succeed, and to believe otherwise is the surest sign we've gotten caught in the snare of perfectionism.

Perfectionism is a sort of disease, part of a syndrome resulting from what I often describe as *cultural stress*. This stress stems from a culture that places too many demands on us. There are meetings we must attend, emails we must read, cell phone calls we must answer, meals we must plan, bills we must pay, gifts we must buy—even the day-to-day stuff can place a heavy load of stress on our shoulders. Add to that all the bad news on radio and television, the noise we encounter everywhere we go, the traffic jams, and the crowds—and the stress really piles up. We think that somehow we must deal with all of this and also be perfect in every way, but of course, we can't. This makes us pessimistic, and we begin to believe we're just not good enough.

So how do we fix this? How do we deal with the cultural stress/perfectionism syndrome? First and most importantly, we have to reject the very idea of perfection. It is important to understand that, yes, you want to do things as well as you can, but you can't expect to do them *perfectly*. Remember? Perfection is impossible. So you should strive for *excellence*, not perfection.

Let go of perfectionism and be kinder to yourself. Don't second guess yourself all the time and say, "I should have done this or I shouldn't have done that." Don't be your own harshest critic. If you are, you'll never be really successful.

To reduce cultural stress and to be more successful, you need to think more and more positively. If you look for improvement and expect it, you are very likely to experience it. If a baseball player thinks he's going to strike out, chances are he will. On the other hand, if he thinks he's going to hit a home run, he's got a much better chance of actually hitting it. Keep in mind that you don't have to hit the ball perfectly to send it flying out of the park. When you learn to accept imperfection, your life will be more nearly perfect and you'll be more likely to live a happier and longer life.

LIFE IS ART

One way to reduce cultural stress and avoid perfectionism is to open up your creativity. Every one of us has a creative drive of some sort. Explore until you discover what yours is, if you haven't already, and find an outlet for it. Set aside some time for art. It doesn't have to be painting, sculpture, or music—any sort of creative activity will do so long as you find it engaging. Likely, you'll discover that when you express yourself creatively, you'll feel better about your day, your surroundings, and yourself.

That's why I included the paintings you see in this book—to encourage you to make creative activities an everyday part of your life, just as

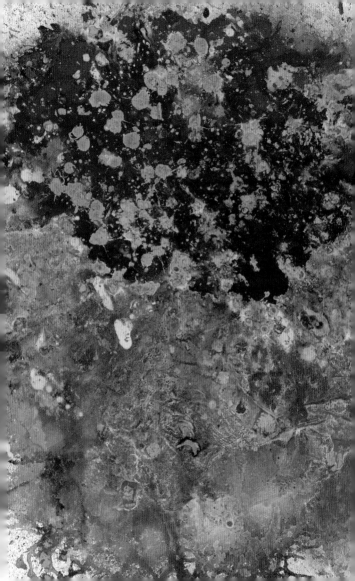

I now make them part of mine. A few years ago a personal health crisis caused me to pick up a brush and try my hand at painting. I enjoyed the creative process far more than I ever thought possible. I truly believe that it helped me heal, and it certainly changed my perspective on life and medicine.

Since that time, I've incorporated art into my treatment programs and offered art therapy sessions at my spas and retreats. The results have been impressive. I see that art therapy works, and study after study has shown this to be the case. For this reason, hospitals and clinics across America and the world are beginning to use art therapy to improve the emotional and physical health of their patients.

What art does for me and what I believe it does for my patients is reconnect us to an earlier time in our lives when play was completely free, when self-expression came easily, and when we didn't mind getting a little mud or paint on our hands and faces. Nothing had to be perfect back then. It just had to be what it was.

Unfortunately, most of us begin to lose that sense of freedom and openness as early as the age of two. We are taught to conform, to behave properly, and follow the rules: in short, to color within the lines. In my view, the most important thing to learn from art therapy is that there are no limits. Try not to get stuck painting within the lines. Better still, imagine that there *are no lines*.

As I hope you can see when you look at my paintings, I put no limits on art. When I paint, I make a few marks on a canvas, add some colors, and let a spray of water interact with them in a random way. Often this takes the canvas in a completely unexpected direction. How's it going to turn out? I don't know. I want to be surprised by the result. Sometimes, I am very happily surprised.

You can take this same approach to living your life. Be comfortable with yourself and don't let perfectionism and your fear of failure hold you back. Art is never perfect—it merely *exists*. Once you learn that it's okay to paint outside the lines, your accomplishments will amaze you and others as well.

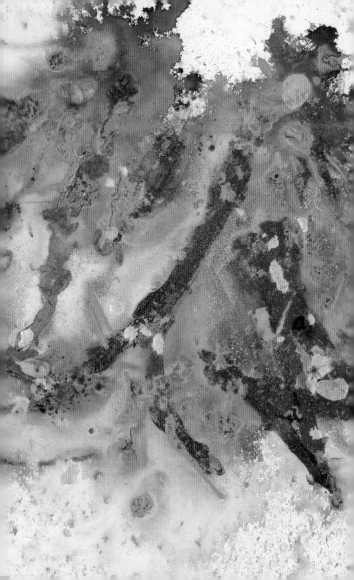

SIMPLE WORDS
OF WISDOM

Occasionally, I have what I believe to be a meaningful insight into the human quest for health and happiness. Usually these insights occur to me when I'm working with patients or talking with a friend, but sometimes they come to mind when I'm painting or just walking from one room into another. If possible, I try to remember them and write them down. Over the years I've collected hundreds of these insights and I now think of them simply as my "sayings."

When patients visit my office to take part in our Inclusive Health program, I share several of the sayings with them. They may focus on one or another of the insights, and sometimes they say, "You know, I haven't thought of that before." It's almost impossible to say which of the insights will attract their interest, and maybe that isn't important since most of the sayings are related in one way or another. They all have in common the idea that you can change your life for the better, that it's all a matter of how you approach the challenges of living. Here are a few insights that I hope will help you accept imperfection and live a longer, happier life.

Die late, not old

Attitude, lifestyle, and good emotional health play a vital role in preventing and treating many types of disease. A positive outlook and healthy lifestyle will also help you look and feel much younger. If you modify your lifestyle by eating better, reducing stress, keeping out of harsh sunlight, using appropriate skin care products, and living a happier life, you'll look many years younger than most people your age. In fact, looking your age or looking much younger is really a matter of choice. It's up to you.

Beware of creating
your own cultural stress

Traffic jams, appointments, deadlines, emails, cell phone calls, and distressing news in the media generate an enormous amount of stress that can, and all too often does, make us unhappy and sick. To avoid this cultural stress and reduce the toll it takes on our emotional and physical health, we must simplify our lives. You may discover that you can live very simply and very well without giving up anything that really matters to you.

**Many of life's most important lessons
are taught by mistakes we have made**

Instead of trying to lay the blame on someone else, take responsibility for your mistakes and learn from them. It's easy to complain about others, but that's a very destructive way of dealing with personal or professional difficulties. You won't solve many problems that way, and you won't learn anything either. If you let them, your mistakes may just become your very best teachers.

Don't let failures spoil your success

No endeavor is ever perfectly successful. We may try to be perfect but, of course, perfection is imaginary. It is impossible in the real world. When we strive for perfection, we are likely to lose sight of our successes and end up feeling as if we have failed. Naturally, you want to do things as well as you can, but strive for excellence, not perfection. That way you can celebrate success when it comes and feel like what you really are—a winner.

Opportunity comes to those who ask

To find the opportunities that really pay off, you have to knock on doors and make calls. In other words, you have to ask for what you want. Never be afraid to ask. You may be very happily surprised by the results.

Be brave enough to make difficult decisions

Obviously, making the wrong decision can have unfortunate consequences, but making no decision at all might be even worse. Decisions have to be made all the time. If we can't make them, we'll be paralyzed both in business and in our personal lives. Decision making takes guts. You have to be brave and determined enough to make them.

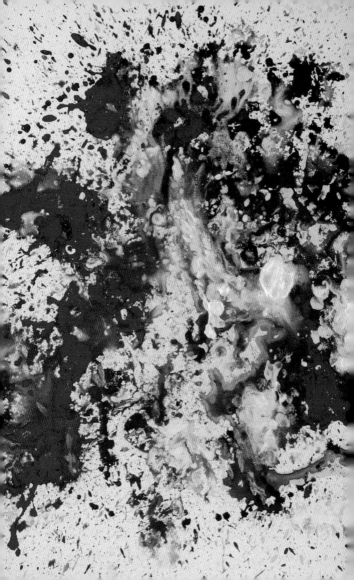

Accept the possibility that
your expectations won't be met

Most dreams are never fulfilled. Sometimes you set goals for yourself that are unattainable and may always be out of reach. Likely you'll never be the richest person in the world—there is always somebody richer. Likely you'll never be the fastest runner in the world—there is always somebody faster. It's very unhealthy and unhelpful to measure yourself against goals that are either out of reach or out of the realm of possibility. It's usually best not to measure yourself against the achievements of others at all. Instead, set reasonable goals of your own and measure yourself against those. Then, if your expectations are not met, you can always try again.

If you keep banging your head against the wall, you will get a headache

If things are going badly and it seems that you keep running into a stone wall, maybe it is time to take a detour. Having a wonderful day or a terrible day is less a matter of circumstances than it is of choice. If you keep banging your head against that wall, you are sure to get a headache and have a very bad day no matter how many pain relievers you take. Why not back away from the trouble and have a good day instead?

Listen to yourself so you can pay attention to your needs

Our bodies have lots of important things to tell us. But all too often we're not paying attention. We're just not listening. For instance, we may be under too much stress, working too hard, or eating all the wrong things. Even though our bodies are crying out for change, we have no idea there's a problem.

Don't let overeating become a substitute for proper cultural stress management

Everyday life can be stressful, with hundreds of things demanding our attention. This sort of cultural stress can produce high levels of anxiety and it can even lead to a type of attention deficit disorder. It can also cause us to eat unhealthy foods and gain weight. When people are anxious they tend to overeat and ignore the health implications of their diet. Keep stress and anxiety levels under control and you'll not only eat better, you'll look better and feel better, too.

Eat to hydrate your brain, allowing happiness to enter

A major health concern today is the food we eat, which is said to contain too many calories, too much fat, and too little real nutrition. I believe a far more important issue is the lack of moisture in our diet.

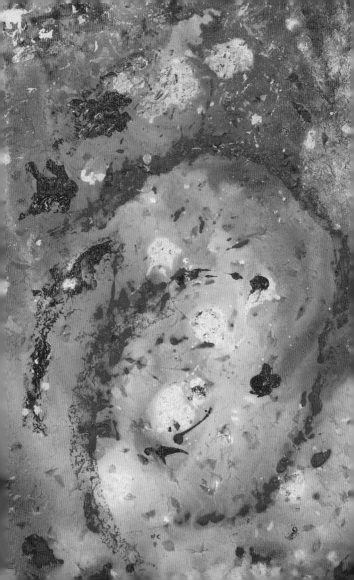

Our food is too dry and does not contain nearly enough structural water. We need to eat more water-rich foods to keep our cells well hydrated and healthy. And it's a lot easier to be happy when you're healthy.

Eat your medicine

Eating the right food can be the best medicine you'll ever take. You've probably heard you should drink eight glasses of water a day, but unfortunately, that won't do much to improve your health. When you drink that much water, it'll just run right through you without adding any of the critical moisture your cells need to survive. To properly hydrate your cells, you need to eat lots of raw fruits and vegetables containing the structural water your body requires. Structural water is absorbed slowly and retained in our cells. These same raw fruits and vegetables contain healthful antioxidants and roughage to eliminate fat and help your body guard against bone loss and cancer. Eating more produce will also help you lose weight. The pounds may just drop away without you even noticing.

Returning to your youth
is the path to happiness

Many people equate happiness with financial success or luxurious surroundings. While money may purchase a semblance of happiness for some, rich people are often no happier than their less prosperous friends and associates. Happiness eludes them because they have allowed themselves to grow old inside and outside as well. For most of us, the surest path to happiness is a return to our youth. No, we can't actually roll back the years, but we can recapture the open, inquiring, and carefree attitudes of the young along with the joys that accompany them.

Give yourself permission to be successful

People measure success in many different ways. Some measure it by the size of the salary they earn or the cost of the car they drive. Others measure it by the amount of power, stock, or money they can accumulate. Still others measure it by winning in sports or other types of competition. But real success comes when you are able to accomplish what others believed was impossible. So think out of the box and give yourself permission to try something that no one else has attempted. Even you may not be fully aware of your own hidden potential.

DR. HOWARD MURAD'S INCLUSIVE HEALTH APPROACH

A prominent Los Angeles physician, Dr. Howard Murad has successfully treated over 50,000 patients. Drawing on his training as both a pharmacist and physician, he has developed a popular and highly effective line of skin care products that has won praise from health- and beauty-conscious people everywhere. A practitioner not just of medicine but of the philosophy of health, he has written dozens of books and articles, earning him a worldwide reputation as an authority on slowing the aging process.

Dr. Murad's unique approach to medicine involves a concept he calls Inclusive Health. An alternative to traditional medical practice with its emphasis on the "spot treatment" of individual conditions or illnesses, the Inclusive Health approach treats the whole patient. Among other things, it takes into consideration the patient's diet, lifestyle, and emotional state as well as intercellular water—the hydration level of cells.

Years of painstaking research and experience with thousands of patients have shown Dr. Murad that human health and happiness are directly linked to the ability of cells to retain water. A poor diet and the stress of day-to-day living can damage the all-important membranes that form cell walls. Over time, the membranes become broken and porous, causing the cells to leak water and lose vitality. This in turn leads to accelerated aging and a wide variety of diseases and syndromes.

In his groundbreaking bestseller *The Water Secret*, published in 2010, Dr. Murad outlined how to stop this process—and reverse it—through Inclusive Healthcare. This approach has three essential components. The first involves good skin care practices; the second, a healthy diet emphasizing raw fruits and vegetables; and the third an overall reduction in stress combined with a more youthful and creative outlook on life.

The third component, which emphasizes our emotional state, may be the most challenging part of the Inclusive Health treatment process for people to adopt. The breakneck pace of modern life with its freeways, computers, cell phones, and fast-paced living places upon us an enormous amount of what Dr. Murad describes as *cultural stress.*

To deal with this runaway stress, we live increasingly structured lives that are less and less open to the free play and creativity that make life worth living. *We can choose not to live this way.* But reducing stress and embracing a more youthful outlook often involves major shifts in lifestyle—changes in jobs, accommodations, locales, hobbies, habits, and relationships. It may even require a complete personal transformation of the sort sometimes identified with a single galvanizing moment of self-awareness. You may experience a transforming moment like that while walking on a beach, creating a work of art, driving through the countryside, or maybe just stretching your arms after a long night's sleep. Who can say?

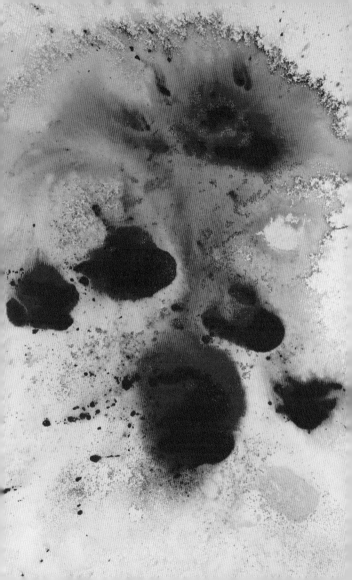

To help his patients awaken to a better life Dr. Murad has composed a substantial collection of personal insights or sayings that deliver bits of health advice, philosophy, and wisdom straight up, like strong coffee. In his medical practice, Dr. Murad shares these brief meditations with patients as a way of encouraging them to improve their health by adopting more youthful, creative, and health-conscious lifestyles. You may find them similarly inspirational. In addition to the insights you have already encountered in this book, here are a few others that you may find interesting and useful.

To reach your full potential, live in a physically and emotionally healthy environment.

*Dance even when you
can't hear the music.*

———————————

*Allow your disabilities to
promote your abilities.*

———————————

Forgive yourself.

———————————

*Rewrite and reframe
the negatives in your life.*

———————————

*Real change only happens
when you create your own.*

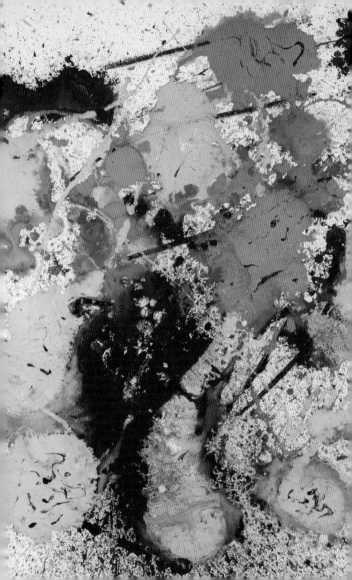

*You are responsible only
for your own problems.*

---

*Progress starts when you
cut the umbilical cord.*

Allow yourself to speak.

Inspiration before perspiration.

---

*Feel that you are about
to improve and you will.*

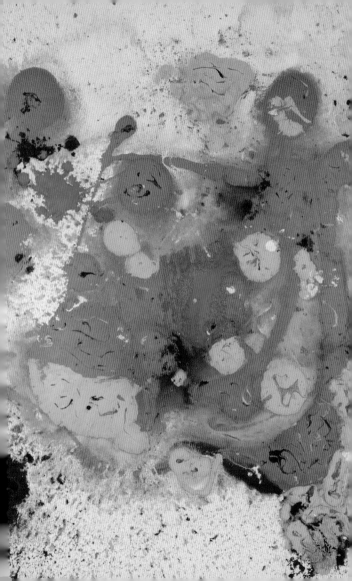

*Be brave enough to expose
yourself to your harshest critic
without fear of rejection.*

———————————

*When your expectations are not met,
think of it as an opportunity.*

———————————

*Make transitions into an
opportunity for positive change.*

———————————

*The least of us may become
the best of us.*

———————————

*When you are happy, your loved
ones will be happy.*

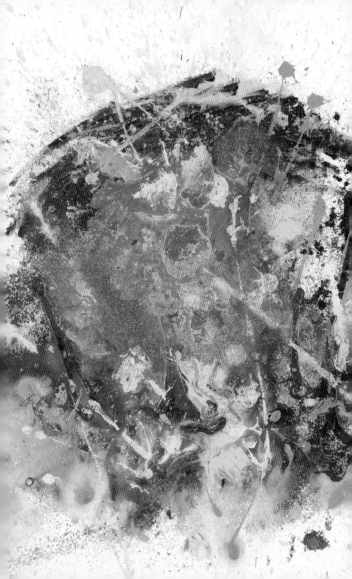

It's not the stress —
but how you respond to it.

———————————————

Project happiness.

———————————————

Reduce the number
of your daily decisions.

———————————————

To reach your potential,
you must risk failure.

———————————————

Make your mark, but allow the
canvas of life to direct you.

Dear reader,
Please share this book with others or give it as a gift to family, friends, or business associates. Also be sure to look for Dr. Murad's other inspirational "little" books:

One Key Can Open Many Doors

Give Yourself Permission to Be Happy

Honor Yourself

The Best Is Yet to Come

Why Have a Bad Day
When You Can Have a Good Day?